SACRED
PARENTING

T0045759

PARTICIPANT'S GUIDE

Books by Gary Thomas

Authentic Faith

The Beautiful Fight

Devotions for a Sacred Marriage

Devotions for Sacred Parenting

The Glorious Pursuit

Not the End but the Road

Pure Pleasure

Sacred Influence

Sacred Marriage

Sacred Parenting

Sacred Pathways

Thirsting for God

SACRED PARENTING

HOW RAISING CHILDREN SHAPES OUR SOULS

PARTICIPANT'S GUIDE

GARY THOMAS

ZONDERVAN.com/
AUTHORTRACKER
follow your favorite authors

ZONDERVAN

Sacred Parenting Participant's Guide
Copyright © 2010 by Gary Thomas

Requests for information should be addressed to:

Zondervan, *Grand Rapids, Michigan 49530*

ISBN 978-0-310-32946-6

Cover design: Jeff Gifford
Cover photography: Larry Forsstedt, Folio
Interior design: Ben Fetterley

Printed in the United States of America

HB 11.21.2023

CONTENTS

Introduction:
Never Wait for a Parking Place

The young family, with their three children under the age of six, wore their weariness like coal miners returning home from the mines. Their shoulders were hunched over, their eyes sagged, even their breathing seemed labored.

I learned a valuable lesson watching them: it's not worth it to wait for them to pack up their groceries and get their three children strapped into safety seats so they can finally vacate their parking place. You'll feel like you need a nap just watching them. It's best to just drive on and find another open space.

Whenever I speak to young families, I encourage them with the words that there are seasons of liberation up ahead. The first such season occurs when you finally divorce yourself from the ten-pound diaper bag. There's a great deal of freedom when you can leave the house without half a Walmart store hanging on your shoulder.

The second stage of liberation occurs when the kids can take a shower or bath on their own. You can actually *sit down* for ten minutes and your kids still come out clean! You may have a bathroom in serious need of tidying up afterward, but hey, at least you were able to catch your breath. This season often gives you the opportunity (should you choose to take advantage of it) to cut your daily coffee intake by half.

The next liberating moment is when you can leave the kids home without a babysitter. Ah, it's a truly glorious evening when you don't have to tack on the expense of a babysitter who expects a contribution to her IRA every time she watches television with your kids. One time, when my wife and I calculated what the babysitter and movie tickets would cost, we figured that the best movie in the history of the world couldn't possibly be worth that much, particularly when the DVD would be out in six months. We might have been shortsighted in our view, but I can now understand how other couples in the same situation have come to a similar conclusion. That's why it's so liberating when one of the kids is old enough to watch the others, at least for a few hours.

Finally, the day will come when your kids can actually *drive themselves* to school and school-related events. When you cease being a taxi driver, you can actually take up a hobby, start to work out again, or even read a book! You and your spouse can reconnect in new ways, and the day may even come when you're able to have sexual relations without anyone else being in the house, and you don't have to worry about being overheard.

It will feel so liberating, like an afternoon nap, until . . .

Until you get to be where my wife and I are right now. Lisa and I are just a few months removed from becoming "empty nesters." We can hardly believe that the season of active, everyday parenting is coming to an end. Believe it or not, part of us wishes we could start over at the diaper-changing stage and do it all over again. We've probably forgotten how tiring each stage was, but we're well aware of how much it hurts to watch your children slowly leave you behind.

Take a Step Back

Whatever stage of parenting you find yourself in, each season provides spiritual blessings and benefits that many Christians remain unaware of. It's my belief that family life is one of the most spiritually formative experiences in all of human existence.

Accordingly, this study will not provide "five steps to cure toddler temper tantrums," "four ways to get your children to eat some kind of food that actually grows," or "eight steps to get your daughter to decide to marry someone who has a job." Instead, we're going to explore how God uses the process of parenting to change *the parent*.

It's my prayer that by applying a new spiritual sensitivity to the everyday trials and challenges of parenting, you'll mature and grow in amazing new ways, becoming a little more like Christ, on a daily basis. Whether you need to learn how to handle your anger, become more patient, develop the skills of a listener, learn to manage your priorities better, or become more courageous, parenting is an ideal arena to learn all of these lessons, and many more.

Let's begin!

OF NOTE

Quotations interspersed throughout each session of this participant's guide are excerpts from the book *Sacred Parenting* by Gary Thomas (Zondervan, 2004).

SESSION 1

Parenting: God's Hammer on Our Souls

God can use the difficulties, challenges, struggles, and joys of parenting to help us become more like Christ.

Introduction

Have you ever seen a blacksmith massage a horseshoe to get it to take shape?

Of course not. He heats it up, hammers it, bends it, does all kinds of things to get the metal to become what he needs and wants it to be.

The Bible compares blacksmiths working on metal to God working on our souls. Consider the following:

For you, O God, tested us; you refined us like silver.... We went through fire and water, but you brought us to a place of abundance. (Psalm 66:10 – 12)

This third I will bring into the fire; I will refine them like silver and test them like gold. (Zechariah 13:9)

He will sit as a refiner and purifier of silver; he will purify the Levites and refine them like gold and silver. (Malachi 3:3)

The purifying process can be painful, confusing, and heartrending, but it's essential, for one significant reason: we're not as mature as God wants us to be. None of us is. Don't get me wrong. God loves us. He accepts us in Christ. He is even pleased with us and *delights* in us. But in the midst of that love, acceptance, and forgiveness, he desires for us to become ever more like Christ.

Here's something you may not have thought of: letting us become parents is one of God's primary methods of sanctification. If you went through my *Sacred Marriage* video curriculum, you heard me talk about how perhaps God designed marriage to make us holy more than to make us happy. This concept takes on an entirely new flavor when applied to parenting.

You see, within marriage, you ultimately choose what you're willing to live with. If you marry an angry person, you know you'll have to learn how to deal with your spouse's anger. If you marry a passive person, or a fearful person, or an impulsive person, in the end you have to admit that you chose this person, and in choosing that person, you chose your future battles.

With kids, it's a bit different. They come out ready-made with spiritual challenges we can't even imagine beforehand. And God has this brilliant ability to place a child in a family who happens to push *just the right buttons* to get under the skin of Mom or Dad (or both).

The potential for spiritual growth in such a setting is enormous.

Before You Watch the Video

Take turns discussing one character trait you've improved on since you've become a parent. Has raising children had anything to do with that character growth?

DVD TEACHING NOTES

A few verses and a thousand books

Spiritual growth through family life

An active pursuit of Christlikeness
2 Corinthians 7:1 — "Dear friends, let us purify ourselves from everything that contaminates body and spirit, perfecting holiness out of reverence for God."

Parenting puts the spotlight on our weaknesses — "We can choose to let sin tear apart our families, or we can use our families to tear apart our sin."

Role models
How our children "study" us

Paul and Timothy

1 Timothy 4:16 — "Watch your life and doctrine closely. Persevere in them, because if you do, you will save both yourself *and your hearers.*" (emphasis added)

1 Timothy 4:15 — "Be diligent in these matters; give yourself wholly to them, *so that everyone may see your progress.*" (emphasis added)

Cathy, Gordon, and Matt

DVD Discussion

1. Why do you think the Bible is relatively silent on the issue of "how-to" parenting? How does this compare with the numerous Christian books published on the topic?

2. No doubt parenting has challenged you in many ways, but have you ever considered the spiritual benefit that can result from it? Have you ever actively sought to learn spiritual lessons while raising your children? If so, give one or two examples.

3. Gary suggests that Christians, by and large, don't live with the urgency that Paul speaks of in 2 Corinthians 7:1, about earnestly purifying ourselves from everything that contaminates body and spirit. Do you agree? If so, why do you think this is, and what can the church do about it?

4. Have you ever seen your kids pick up on something you do or say and copy it? Give some examples. What did you learn from those encounters?

Why does parenting necessitate purifying ourselves? Because our children frequently follow the ruts we lay down.

5. Reread 1 Timothy 4:15 – 16. Discuss how focusing on our own spiritual growth can actually benefit our children's spiritual growth.

6. Have you ever known someone who was raising a child like Matt? What are the particular lessons that difficult children can teach us?

7. How can parents maintain an attitude of gratitude and appreciation for their children in the face of the many disappointments that often accompany parenting?

8. Discuss Gary's final question: name a particular parental challenge that you're facing with one of your kids, and then talk about how *you*, personally, need to grow to help your child mature in this area.

We need to use the most wearisome aspects of parenting as the occasion for thanking God for putting up with us. When we look through this lens, we find that raising a demanding child can actually become motivation for worshiping and adoring God.

CLOSING

Take time as a group (or as couples) to pray in some of the following directions:

- "Father, thank you for giving us the particular children you've placed in our home. We believe you are a God of providence, and whether we gave birth to these children or welcomed them through adoption, we trust that you knew what you were doing when you called us to become our children's parents."
- "Lord, open our eyes to our own weaknesses in the coming days; show us where we have not purified ourselves from everything that contaminates body and spirit, and give us a renewed desire to become more like Christ."
- Pray for those couples who need special encouragement and/or who currently feel overwhelmed by the parenting challenges they are facing on a daily basis.

BETWEEN SESSIONS

On your own, or as a couple, read the following devotion in the next couple of days to further reflect on the lessons you have learned in this session.

DEVOTION: GOING AGAINST THE GRAIN

"For the grace of God that brings salvation has appeared to all men. It teaches us to say 'No' to ungodliness and worldly passions, and to live self-controlled, upright and godly lives in this present age, while we wait for the blessed hope – the glorious appearing of our great God and Savior, Jesus Christ, who gave himself for us to redeem us from all wickedness and to purify for himself a people that are his very own, eager to do what is good." (Titus 2:11 – 14)

Dr. James Dobson tells of the time that he was talking to a college senior about her graduation plans. As they discussed various vocational opportunities, the young woman lowered her voice, looked over her shoulder, and whispered, "May I be completely honest with you?"

Dr. Dobson answered, "Sure, Debbie. You can say anything you want."

"I don't want to have a career at all. What I really want is to be a full-time wife and mother."

"Why do you say that like it's some kind of secret?" Dr. Dobson asked. "It's your life. What's wrong with doing whatever you want with it?"

"Are you kidding? If my professors and my classmates knew that's what I wanted, they'd laugh me out of school."[1]

There's no getting around the fact that leaving the workplace and being in the home full-time is risking some status in the world's view. Our society has undergone a massive sociological shift; we are no longer given esteem by what we are, character-wise, but by what we do vocationally. A man might engage in sexual play with a woman young enough to be his daughter and habitually cheat on his wife, but if he's president of the United States and satisfies certain political expectations, he remains the media's darling. A woman might be materialistic, selfish, and vain, but if she's beautiful and makes movies, she's likely to be adored and pampered and even, sadly, emulated by young girls.

Conversely, a brilliant woman, easily capable of getting a PhD in quantum physics or researching a cure for breast cancer, who chooses to homeschool her children still has to work with a "suspicious" school district that wonders if she's truly "qualified" to teach her children by herself, since, after all, she's not a member of the teacher's union.

A very insightful stay-at-home woman with much to say will likely have to endure mountains of rejection slips before she finds a book publisher willing to take a chance on her, while a woman who starts a cookie company or who becomes a movie star or singer will have publishers begging her to write her life story.

There's no getting around it: contemporary culture values what we do outside the home. This means it takes a good deal of courage for both men and women to go against the grain and take on the commitment of parenting. I know a man who sacrificed considerably to get through a prestigious law school and landed a job with a solid law firm, only to find that as a young lawyer, you are only as popular as the number of hours you bill. He had a choice to make: keep working toward becoming a partner in the law firm, or grow up influencing his kids and never being fully esteemed at work. He chose to stay connected to his children, realizing that eventually that would mean finding a new employer.

Even our children may ridicule our choice to focus on home. Writer Carolyn Mahaney tells of the time that one of her daughters "despised" her for having "thrown her life away" by staying at home instead of making a name for herself in the world. Eventually, that daughter radically changed her mind and repented of what she now calls her "greatest sin." Carolyn's faithfulness in living an upright and godly life, and saying "no" to worldly passions, won over her daughter by example.

Writer Iris Krasnow, the mother of four boys, admits that as a young woman, she looked down on the very thing she had now become—a woman dedicated first and foremost to her children. What Iris eventually found, however, is that by forfeiting society's definition of esteem, she "found her soul." She imagines what it would be like to have a twenty-one-year-old daughter, and what she would tell her if she was as eager as Iris had been to make a name for herself: "I would reveal that when I was her age I wanted to be stronger and smarter than my housewife mother, that my outrage at the oppression of women stuck in their kitchens helped turn me into a savvy Woman of the World who was determined never to become stagnant and subservient.... I grew into a woman ablaze with ambition who was always racing past the Now to try and get somewhere better, a woman who was after the perfect job, the perfect body, and the perfect relationship all at once.... Then I would tell my daughter that no matter how high I climbed, what I craved in the deepest cave of my heart was a good man to marry and to have a bunch of kids."[2]

It's difficult, isn't it, not to be weighted down, or at least influenced, by a constant barrage of messages that stand in direct contradiction and defiance of a life focused on what happens at home. The so-called "traditional" family has now become the "radical" family, or the "behind-the-times" family — but regardless of what it's called, for most of us, it's God's best plan for our lives as he seeks to "redeem us from all wickedness and to purify for himself a people that are his very own, eager to do what is good."

This isn't to deny that many women must work as well as parent. The Bible specifically references women who work. I recently received a heartfelt email from a woman who asked me to pray for her and other African-American wives; she said that she didn't know any wives in her community who could afford to be stay-at-home moms, even if they wanted to be. This puts additional stress on them and their marriages.

Whatever the employment situation, it's best for a child to grow up with both a father and a mother who stay married and who are radically invested in their family's emotional and spiritual welfare. Life isn't tidy; we can't always give our kids the ideal, but that doesn't mean we shouldn't aspire toward the ideal. This aim, in and of itself, will demand great sacrifice, loads of humility, deep wisdom, and a discernment that embraces the message of God's Word while saying "no" to the message of popular culture.

Let us remember that Jesus gave himself for us to redeem us from all wickedness — and that includes materialism, pride, and the pursuit of selfish power and empty fame — and to purify for himself a people that are his very own, eager to do what is good — and that includes learning to serve, love, and sacrifice on our family's behalf.

What is active parenting, truly involved parenting, calling you to embrace and grow toward today? What do we, as parents, need to become to complete this task?

RECOMMENDED READING

In preparation for session 2, please read chapter 1 of Gary Thomas's book Sacred Parenting, *"Papa God."*

Notes

SESSION 2

IT'S ALL ABOUT HIM:
GOD-CENTERED PARENTING

The "earthy" process of changing diapers, educating toddlers, and raising teens is actually a sacred enterprise and a continual act of worship.

INTRODUCTION

A friend of mine went to Italy and brought back a present for me: a small plastic figurine of a (as she put it) "bald Francis." That tiny figurine has watched over my desk as I've written my last three books. I still have a bit more hair than he does, but not much.

My friend knows of my appreciation for the life of Francis of Assisi. She has spoken with me many times also of my fondness for John of the Cross and Teresa of Avila, who lived several hundred years after Francis, but who, with a chaste relationship, fathered and mothered the "discalced Carmelites" and brought reform to a lapsed system of monks and nuns.

She has also heard me speak of John Climacus, the stalwart chronicler of Eastern Orthodox spirituality, who lived five hundred years before Francis and who wrote *the* manual on spiritual growth for early monks. Or go back earlier still, and we can read the account of Antony of Egypt, whose sojourn into the desert spawned a movement of hermetic spirituality that marked the church for several centuries.

Why is it, when thinking of people who exhibit exceptional holiness, that we tend to be drawn to *celibate* heroes and heroines? Today, some might, to their credit, think of Billy Graham, a married man with children, but even in this instance, recognition would likely be given primarily for what he did outside the home, not in it. Why is that? Is there really no place in the church to universally celebrate the sanctified mother and father of children?

For us to be successful in parenting, I believe we must see our job as a sacred enterprise; we may not have the leisure to spend hours a day in prayer like a monk might, but changing dirty diapers, teaching a toddler to be less selfish, explaining the way of faith to a preadolescent, and helping a teenager grow into a productive member of God's kingdom are just as legitimate acts of worship.

We don't have to *make* family life sacred; it *is* sacred. The only question is, do we treat it as such?

BEFORE YOU WATCH THE VIDEO

Spend some time discussing your typical thoughts when you enter a church sanctuary. What's going through your mind? Now compare and contrast your typical thoughts when you walk into your kitchen or living room, or through the front door of your house. With those comparisons in mind, turn on the video.

DVD TEACHING NOTES

Why do we become parents?
Malachi 2:15 — "Has not the Lord made them one? In flesh and spirit they are his. And why one? *Because he was seeking godly offspring.*" (emphasis added)

From dysfunction to redemption

The promise: "He will turn the hearts of the fathers to their children, and the hearts of the children to their fathers." (Malachi 4:6)

The Genesis problem: dysfunctional families

• Adam and Eve

• Cain and Abel

• Noah and his son (9:24)

• Abraham and his son (ch. 16)

• Lot and his daughters (19:36)

• Jacob and Esau (ch. 27)

• Joseph's brothers (ch. 37)

In our families, we are invited to live out the _____.
In other words, having kids isn't about _____. It's about
_____. We are called to bear and raise children for _____
_____.

Reverence for God
2 Corinthians 7:1

James 3:2

A "child-centered parent" versus a "God-centered parent"

When we know the _____, we will endure the _____.

White spots
"For I was hungry and you gave me something to eat, I was thirsty and you gave me something to drink, I was a stranger and you invited me in, I needed clothes and you clothed me, I was sick and you looked after me." (Matthew 25:35 – 36)

DVD DISCUSSION

1. Discuss openly and honestly the reasons you decided to conceive or adopt children.

> *The best reason to have kids — the one reason that will last beyond mere sentiment — is so simple that it might not seem very profound: God commands us to have children (Genesis 1:28). It's his desire that we "be fruitful and increase in number." ... In other words, having kids isn't about us — it's about him. We are called to bear and raise children for the glory of God.*

2. How will the biblical understanding of conceiving and raising children for the glory of God affect your parenting practices in the future?

3. What hope can Christian parents receive from the promise of Malachi 4:6?

4. How does living by the gospel cause us to view parenting differently than it was viewed by our Old Testament ancestors?

5. Reread James 3:2, and then read Romans 7:14–20. How should the biblical teaching on the reality of indwelling sin affect the way we deal with our children's acts of disobedience?

6. Describe the common traits of a "child-centered" parent. Now discuss the characteristics of someone you would consider a "God-centered" parent. What are the differences? How can we become more like the latter, and less like the former, in the way we treat our own families?

7. Read Matthew 25:35–36. Have you ever considered how these verses might apply to a mom or dad taking in a newborn baby? How might meditating on Christ's gratitude in this passage reflect on the way you view your parental obligations and duties?

We live in the midst of holy teachers. Sometimes they spit up on themselves or us. Sometimes they throw tantrums. Sometimes they cuddle us and kiss us and love us. In the good and bad they mold our hearts, shape our souls, and invite us to experience God in newer and deeper ways.

CLOSING

Take time as a group (or as couples) to pray in some of the following directions:

- "Father, forgive us for the selfish reasons that led us to become parents. Help us to exchange reasons such as _____, _____, and _____, and embrace your desire that we raise godly offspring out of reverence for you."
- "Lord, thank you for sending your messenger and for giving us your Holy Spirit so that our dysfunctional family might become a picture (however imperfect) of your redemptive and reconciling work in the world. We thank you that we have available to us your power, your presence, your guidance, your comfort, your counsel, and your companionship as we raise our children together — with you."
- "Our Father, help us remember that we *all* stumble in many ways — including our children. Please help us to respond to their struggles against sin with godly grace and with the hope of your forgiveness and redemption."
- "Lord, the next time we view parenting as a heavy burden, please give us an attitude of worship, remembering that when we give our infant a bath, we are washing your baby; when we feed a hungry six-year-old, we are feeding your child; and when we comfort a hurting adolescent, we are encouraging your teen."

BETWEEN SESSIONS

On your own, or as a couple, read the following devotion in the next couple of days to further reflect on the lessons you have learned in this session.

DEVOTION: THE "NOBLEST AND MOST PRECIOUS" WORK

"Bring the boy to me." (Mark 9:19)

As we discussed in this session, people choose to have children (or not to have children) for the flimsiest of reasons: because we want to carry on the family name, because we desire to experience the intimate parent/ child relationship, because we want someone there for us in our old age, because we fear we would feel lonely without children. Whatever your reasoning might have been, this is key: our motivation to be a parent will dramatically shape our actions as parents. If my goal is simply to raise "happy" children, I'll buy them whatever they want instead of teaching them to be responsible and generous with money. If my goal is to have "successful" children, I will spare no expense helping them to rise above others—they'll get the best coaching, the best equipment, maybe even the services of a sports psychologist. I'll act as if the most important thing in the world is that they get into the right school, take the right classes, and get the right diploma, so that they can get a job with the right firm, the right company, in the right industry.

But Christian parenting calls us to a much different purpose and motivation: raising servants who will seek first the kingdom of God. This doesn't mean we don't emphasize education and training, as it honors God to help our children become all that he wants them to be. But as we read in the book of Malachi, God is seeking godly offspring. That's one of the reasons God wants us to work on our marriages—godly marriages are far more likely to produce godly children. Unstable, chaotic, and "serial" marriages often produce troubled kids—and that's not the offering God wants from us.

Malachi also gives us a picture of what a godly child is: "[Levi] revered me and stood in awe of my name. True instruction was in his mouth and nothing false was found on his lips. He walked with me in peace and uprightness, and turned many from sin" (Malachi 2:5-6).

According to this passage, God wants us to maintain families that teach our daughters and sons to

- live in awe of him,
- revere his Word,
- walk with God in fellowship,
- live peacefully with others, and
- turn others from their sin.

When I seek to raise children for the glory of God, I'll be willing to face the difficult realities of training, correcting, encouraging, praying, and the like, because I know there's no higher end, no more important use of my time, no greater good than that I should raise godly children. While I'll still want them to develop their abilities, I'll be equally concerned about their character and their passion for God's work. Almost five hundred years ago, Martin Luther wrote, "But the greatest good in married life, that which makes all suffering and labor worthwhile, is that God grants offspring and commands that they be brought up to worship and serve him. In all the world this is the noblest and most precious work, because to God there can be nothing dearer than the salvation of souls."[1]

I'll be honest: I didn't know this when I first had kids. But whatever our initial reasons for choosing to have kids, what matters now is our current motivation. What is the grand scheme behind your family? What will motivate you to train and instruct your children instead of ignoring something because you're too tired, too distracted, or too fearful to address it? What greater end will fuel your efforts?

On one occasion in the New Testament, a deeply troubled boy proves too difficult for the disciples to handle. His father appeals directly to Jesus, and Jesus says with all his authority, "Bring the boy to me" (Mark 9:19).

Those five words have filled my mind for over a decade as a parent. It is what we are called to do, as far as it depends on us, for our sons and our daughters: bring them to Christ.

Some children will follow eagerly. Others will overwhelm us with their resistance. But our ultimate aim, our end goal, is listening to Jesus say,

"Bring the boy to me." We can't make them follow Christ, but we can certainly tell them the truth about Christ and model a life of faith that will serve as an invitation to embrace Christ.

Lord, refine our motivations, purify our actions, and energize our hearts so that we will do all that we can to help our children find their greatest joy and their highest aim in serving you.

RECOMMENDED READING

In preparation for session 3, please read chapter 2 of Sacred Parenting, *"The Hardest Hurt of All."*

Notes

SESSION 3

THE HARDEST HURT OF ALL

We must become spiritually strong enough to watch our children hurt, so that they can develop and mature into faithful followers of Christ.

INTRODUCTION

The middle-aged mom cringed when her daughter lost the election to become student body president, just as she had cringed when her daughter didn't get chosen as a cheerleader. But this rejection, one year after the election loss, was more difficult still. In spite of high grades, a decent SAT score, and careful logging of her volunteer hours, the young woman received a small envelope from her college of choice.

This has to be a rejection, Liz thought, but she knew her daughter would want to open the letter herself. *This is going to devastate her.*

Liz spent the entire day in a state of turmoil. She couldn't get anything done. She found herself crying. Her daughter had tried *so hard*, and she wanted this *so much*. It just wasn't fair.

She even had some severe words for God, but we don't need to get into that.

When her daughter got home, Liz handed over the envelope, fighting back the tears. The young woman took the envelope, and from the expression on her face, the mom could tell she knew what it meant. Without saying a word, the daughter went up to her bedroom, closed the door, and stayed there for a good hour.

Now the mom was beside herself. What could she do? What could she say? Finally, she knocked on her daughter's bedroom door.

"Honey? Are you all right?"

Her daughter opened the door with car keys in her hand. "Yeah. I'm going over to Katie's. Bye."

Later that night, Liz called Katie's mom, as her daughter still hadn't said a word about the rejection, other than to confirm it. Katie's mom happened to be a trained counselor, and Liz thought that perhaps, with her daughter having spent the afternoon at her house, the counselor could give her some tips to help Katie get over the disappointment.

"Liz, can I be honest with you?" Katie's mom asked.

"Certainly."

"Your daughter is a happy girl. This wasn't a big deal to her."

"She must be in denial," Liz answered. "I know how much she wanted this."

"No, you know how much *you* wanted it. The only thing that bothers your daughter is that she feels like she's let you down, but it's really not a big deal to *her.*"

Liz was flabbergasted. "Are you telling me she really doesn't care?"

"I'm telling you that she doesn't feel like a failure. She just feels bad that her mom thinks she feels like a failure."

This became a life-altering moment for Liz — an opportunity to critique herself and her emotions; her sense of self and security; and her view of her children, God, and life in entirely new ways. She came to realize she wasn't *raising* Katie as much as she was *depending* on Katie, for her own sense of self-worth, her own feelings of accomplishment, and her own belief in her abilities as a mother.

Parenting has a way of making every one of us parents come face to face with our true motivation, shaky sense of self-worth, and conflicted beliefs about what really matters. One of the greatest spiritual challenges we will ever endure is watching a child fail, get injured, or even die. Just the *threat* of any one of these can paralyze us; their actual occurrence will cast us into the arms of God or tempt us to become angry at God — sometimes both, simultaneously.

Nothing can teach us to trust God quite like being a parent, just as nothing can tempt us toward fear quite as much as being a parent. One thing is certain: we'll leave this relationship radically changed, either better able to critique and master our fears, or even more imprisoned by fear.

BEFORE YOU WATCH THE VIDEO

Describe what it felt like to watch one of your children get rejected, struggle, or fail. What did you do? How did it stretch your own faith to go through this season of parenting?

DVD TEACHING NOTES

Feeding off of fear
Matthew 6:34

Becoming a parent increases the temptation to fear.
Life stage temptations toward fear

The Israelites

Our fears wound our children.

Dr. Melody Rhode: "Children raised under a coddled philosophy that avoids adversity and pain at all costs are likely to be addicted, obese, dependent, suicidal, incapable, and frequently overwhelmed by life. The phrase 'growing pains' goes beyond aching knees to describe aching hearts and disappointed souls — essential experiences on the path toward maturity. If we 'protect' our children from all risk, challenge, and possible rejection, they likely will become developmentally stunted and will therefore remain immature."

Numbers 14:31 – 33 — "As for your children that you said would be taken as plunder, I will bring them in to enjoy the land you have rejected. But you — your bodies will fall in this desert. Your children will be shepherds here for forty years, *suffering for your unfaithfulness*, until the last of your bodies lies in the desert." (emphasis added)

Fear is a great moral failing.

Revelation 21:8 — "But *the cowardly*, the unbelieving, the vile, the murderers, the sexually immoral, those who practice magic arts, the idolaters and all liars — their place will be in the fiery lake of burning sulfur." (emphasis added)

Don't be afraid.

- "Do not be afraid, Abram. I am your shield, your very great reward." (Genesis 15:1)
- "The angel of God called to Hagar from heaven and said to her, 'What is the matter, Hagar? Do not be afraid.'" (Genesis 21:17)
- "An angel of the Lord appeared to him in a dream and said, 'Joseph son of David, do not be afraid.'" (Matthew 1:20)
- "That night the LORD appeared to [Isaac] and said, 'I am the God of your father Abraham. Do not be afraid.'" (Genesis 26:24)
- "Then the LORD said to Joshua, 'Do not be afraid.'" (Joshua 8:1)
- "But the LORD said to [Gideon], 'Peace! Do not be afraid.'" (Judges 6:23)
- "The angel of the LORD said to Elijah, '... do not be afraid.'" (2 Kings 1:15)
- "But the LORD said to me [Jeremiah], 'Do not be afraid.'" (Jeremiah 1:7 – 8)
- "And you, [Ezekiel], do not be afraid of them or their words. Do not be afraid, though briers and thorns are all around you and you live among scorpions." (Ezekiel 2:6)
- "Do not be afraid, Daniel. Since the first day that you set your mind to gain understanding and to humble yourself before your God, your words were heard, and I have come in response to them." (Daniel 10:12)
- "But Jesus ... said to them, 'Take courage! It is I! Don't be afraid.'" (Matthew 14:27)
- "The angel said to the women, 'Do not be afraid.'" (Matthew 28:5)
- "One night the Lord spoke to Paul in a vision: 'Do not be afraid.'" (Acts 18:9)
- "Then he placed his right hand on me [John] and said: 'Do not be afraid. I am the First and the Last.'" (Revelation 1:17)

Martin Luther King Jr.: "You might be 38 years old, as I happen to be. And one day, some great opportunity stands before you and calls you to stand up for some great principle, some great issue. And you refuse because you want to live longer. You're afraid you will lose your job, be criticized or lose popularity, or you're afraid that somebody will stab you, shoot at you or bomb your house; so you refuse to take a stand. Well, you may live until you are 90, but you are just as dead at 38 as you would be at 90. And the cessation of breathing in your life is but the belated announcement of an earlier death of the spirit."

Parenting builds character and prepares us to fulfill God's call on our lives.
What do you aspire to most for your children: comfort or character?

Parenting invites us to become strong enough to be willing to watch our kids hurt, so that we can also watch them mature and make a difference.

If we can learn to manage fear as parents, we can truly "seek first the kingdom of God" and conquer fear in our ministry, our personal interactions, and our service to God.

DVD DISCUSSION

1. How did fear affect you before you became a parent? What were you most afraid of? Did your family of origin seem rattled by fear?

2. What are your two greatest fears as a parent? Has the discussion in this session affected the way you believe you should deal with those fears?

3. Is there any way in which your fear has harmed your children? If so, how can you create a "teachable" moment by addressing this — in an age-appropriate way — with your children (asking for forgiveness, resolving to make a change, etc.)?

To what do you most aspire for your children — comfort or character? On almost a daily basis, we have to choose between the two, as they inevitably come into conflict. Sacred parenting matures the parent by inviting us to choose service and character for our children over pain-free living.

4. Have you ever thought of fear as a "great moral failing"? Discuss the difference between natural fear and fear that becomes sinful. How can we discern which is which?

5. Describe a moment when you failed to step out in ministry or in relationship, primarily out of fear. Looking back on that time, how would you counsel yourself now? What do you wish you had done differently? How might this affect the way you act in the future?

6. Read John 14:27 and then discuss practical ways that Christians can obey Jesus' command, "Do not let your hearts be troubled."

7. When you think about what God is calling you to do now, in any area of your life, is it possible that fear is the only thing holding you back? If so, will you confess that to the group and ask them to pray for you, and maybe even ask someone to hold you accountable?

> *If our kids never hurt; if they never sin but are only "sick"; if they never "fail" but just get "cheated" by an unfair coach, teacher, principal, and so on—they will never sense their need for a Savior.*

CLOSING

Take time as a group (or as couples) to pray in some of the following directions:

- "Father, forgive us for the times we have allowed fear rather than faith to direct our steps. We are truly sorry for not trusting you, and we pray for the grace to take courage in your presence and to trust in your providence in all our future endeavors."
- "Lord, tonight we specifically lay our fears for our children before you. We ask you to help us face _____, _____, and _____."
- "Our Father, if there is any conversation or relational encounter I am avoiding out of fear, or any act of ministry I am letting fear hold me back from, please grant me the courage to take concrete steps in the next day or two toward obedience. Specifically, I pray that you would grant me the courage to _____."
- "Jesus, thank you for promising that your peace will remain with us. Thank you for warning us not to let our hearts be troubled. Our Savior, we ask you to help us make this so. Let us find our refuge in you so that our hearts will not be troubled."

43

BETWEEN SESSIONS

On your own, or as a couple, read the following devotion in the next couple of days to further reflect on the lessons you have learned in this session.

DEVOTION: A GOOD MAN

"[Barnabas] was a good man, full of the Holy Spirit and faith." (Acts 11:24)

"Mark isn't playing?" I asked. "We're going to get killed! What happened?"
    "He got into trouble at school and his parents want to teach him a lesson."
    It was minutes before our then fourteen-year-old son's basketball team played in the Boys and Girls Club championship game. We had already lost to this team twice, and that was with Mark, our best player. Without him, few of us thought we had a chance to compete, much less win. Still, Lisa and I admired the parents' courage in pulling their son out of an event in such a way that would surely leave a lasting impression. These parents chose to put character above achievement.
    About the time of that tournament, I read the sad account of King George II and Queen Caroline who, in the eighteenth century, put British politics in peril with their unabashed shame of their son Frederick, the heir to the throne. In an almost unbelievable maternal attitude, Caroline said of her offspring, "My dear firstborn is the greatest ass, and the greatest liar, and the greatest canaille [i.e., riffraff], and the greatest beast in the whole world, and I most heartily wish he was out of it."[1]
    As Caroline lay dying, her son wished to see her one last time; the queen refused her son's request, saying, "I shall have one comfort in having my eyes eternally closed—I shall never see that monster again."
    George supported his wife's disdain. When told about his son's desire to see his dying mother, George responded, "Bid him go about his business, for his poor mother is not in a condition to see him act his false, whining, cringing tricks now, nor am I in a humour to bear his impertinence."[2]
    Frederick was due to be king—at that historical period, perhaps the highest level of achievement a person could reach in this world. But his future achievement was emptied by his low character. People

disdain wicked kings every bit as much as they disdain wicked thieves or gamblers. It's the character that creates respect, not the achievement or position. (As it turned out, Frederick died before his father and thus never ascended to the throne.)

The Bible labels people in a refreshingly different manner. The book of Acts calls Barnabas, for instance, a "good man, full of the Holy Spirit and faith," yet I'm struck by how little else we know about him. Was Barnabas a carpenter? A shepherd? A farmer? Were his parents poor or affluent? What color hair did he have? Was he heavy or thin? Did he have a good singing voice? How was he athletically?

We don't know—and we never will. In the biblical writer's eyes, all of that is superfluous. What matters most is what we're told: he had sterling character, he was filled with God's Spirit, and he walked by faith.

That's an eternal perspective worth emulating for our own children. As I write this, my children are twenty-three, twenty, and eighteen, but all of them are still completing their education; we don't know what any of them will end up doing vocationally. In a biblical sense, all of that is secondary. Whether they end up teaching, reaching out to Africa (as one is passionate to do), building a business, or selling cars, ultimately they'll be defined by their character and faith.

I'd rather have an honest son who sells used cars and cares for his family than a dishonest, power-hungry, people-using son who pastors a megachurch of 20,000 but treats his wife like dirt. I'd rather have a decent, caring daughter who teaches preschool students how to color between the lines than a ruthless, corner-cutting, narcissistic daughter who becomes CEO of a Fortune 500 company. Of course, there are many very godly, gracious, and virtuous pastors of large churches, just as there are selfless and generous CEOs. It's a false choice to assume our children have to decide between character and achievement—but it's not a false choice to suggest that as parents we ultimately do need to decide which one we'll emphasize as we raise our children. Many times throughout our children's childhood, we'll make little choices that will tell our children what we value most: character or achievement.

That's why Lisa and I applauded the two parents who told their son, "Your character is more important than a basketball game—even the

SACRED PARENTING PARTICIPANT'S GUIDE

championship game. We're more concerned that you learn this lesson than that you grow up thinking you can get away with bad behavior as long as your achievements are above average." The last thing this world needs is another hotshot athlete who thinks the rules don't apply to him.

By the way, in a somewhat shocking upset, my son's team won the championship game. After the contest, another parent smiled and said, "Boy, now Mark is really going to learn a lesson."

The right one, don't you think?

RECOMMENDED READING

In preparation for session 4, please read chapter 10 of Sacred Parenting, *"A Very Boring Chapter of the Bible (That Can Change Your Life Forever)."*

Notes

SESSION 4

EMBRACING OUR INSIGNIFICANCE

Honestly embracing our historical insignificance will free us up to focus on relationships and eternal significance.

INTRODUCTION

Recording artist Billy Joel won six Grammy awards, received twenty-three Grammy nominations, had sixteen albums that went platinum, and totaled sales of over a hundred million — phenomenal for any musician. And yet he said, after being honored by three separate halls of fame, "You can't go home with the Rock and Roll Hall of Fame. You don't get hugged by the Rock and Roll Hall of Fame, and you don't have children with the Rock and Roll Hall of Fame. I want what everybody wants: to love and be loved and to have a family."

Unfortunately, this latter aim has eluded him. In June of 2009, Billy Joel confirmed that he and his third wife had separated.

By Billy's own definition, he hasn't gotten what he has truly wanted — a family that lasts. There are probably more "American Idol" wannabees than we can count who would willingly trade, ahead of time, a family life for a career like Billy's, and yet the man who has lived through such stupendous success has said he'd rather have the family.

I wonder, if Billy could do it all over again, would he tour less and spend more time with any of his three wives? Would he put a little more focus on his first marriage, trying to make it last, and perhaps a little less on his career? Would he really dig in and try to keep things going with Christie Brinkley, his second wife, or Katie Lee, his third?

I don't write any of this to condemn, ridicule, or mock a man I've never met; we don't know why his marriages broke up, and it's certainly not for me to judge. However, I do think his words at the Hall of Fame induction can help us *learn* from his life, perhaps without making the same mistakes. We spend so much effort and energy trying to climb the ladder of success, only to find, at the end, that it feels empty if we don't have anyone to share that success with.

Most of us — myself certainly included — don't have the talent to succeed on a level anywhere near Billy Joel, commercially speaking. I could live a hundred lives and probably still wouldn't sell a hundred million books.

But as I write this, it's one day after my twenty-sixth wedding anniversary, and my wife and I really enjoyed spending a night away together. My son, now twenty, is coming home tomorrow from a New York summer internship to speak at his little sister's high school baccalaureate, and I can't wait to hear what he has to share with the graduating seniors. My oldest daughter is walking around the house wearing a shirt that says "Action for Africa," wondering when she'll get a chance to go back and show God's love to a people she now loves herself.

And I think, while I may not ever sell a hundred million books, there are three kids and a wife who matter more to me than all the books in the world, and I wouldn't trade places with Billy for a second.

In one of his early hits, Billy sang, "I don't want you to tell me it's time to come home," emphatically reminding whoever he was addressing, "This is *my life*." The everyday realities of marriage and family life do call for regular times of sacrifice, self-denial, and an ironclad will to preserve eternal priorities — and many times, that *does* mean coming home when we're asked to. To build a family, instead of singing, "This is *my* life," we need to remind ourselves, "This is *our* life." Any other attitude, and you may, like Billy (as the song ends), "wake up with yourself."

BEFORE YOU WATCH THE VIDEO

Imagine yourself in retirement. What do you want to be true about your life, your history, the priorities you lived with, and the place you find yourself? Give a short description.

DVD TEACHING NOTES

A very boring chapter
Genesis 5:5 – 14

How quickly even the accomplished are forgotten

What matters most
Future generations

The most important thing we do for our children is _____
_____.

Life isn't about trying to become _____ and making
people remember _____; it's about _____
and living to make people remember _____.

Marsha's gifts

DVD DISCUSSION

1. Can anybody name a great-great-grandparent? Beyond that, are you able to tell what their occupation was, whether they were happily married, what church they attended (if any), and their favorite hobby?

2. What is the best way to truly leave a legacy for our great-great-grandchildren? Nothing is guaranteed, but how can we live today in such a way as to increase our chances of influencing future generations?

3. If you were to look honestly at your life, what percentage of your time, energy, and focus is spent demonstrating your own significance, and what percentage is spent living to serve God and make others remember *him*? Are you comfortable with this percentage?

4. With the previous question in mind, name one or two things you may have to give up or reduce in order to organize your life along the lines of the highest priority.

Scripture knows only one hero, and that hero is God. Our so-called search for significance is often a dangerous attempt to steal some of God's glory.... Embrace your insignificance, and let it reestablish your focus. In God's delightful irony, embracing your temporal insignificance leads to the greatest eternal significance.

5. Read Genesis 17:15 – 16. (The name Sarah means "princess.") Why does God choose to bless Sarah? Now read Genesis 18:19. What do these passages teach us about our priorities as parents, and about what God is seeking from us in return for everything he has given us, beginning with our families?

6. Consider this quote from the book *Sacred Parenting*: "What popular society values most grows irrelevant and even comical when confronted by the inexorable weight of history." How, as parents, can we communicate this truth to our children, who are immersed in popular culture from an early age? How do we transfer this value and perspective so that they don't waste their lives on the trivial?

7. If you were facing a terminal illness, as Marsha did, what words would you want to share with your children and what activities would you want to enjoy with your family while there was still time? How can this list direct your actions over the course of the next year?

Sacred parenting calls us to focus our brief lives on what will create the most impact for future generations. We will soon be forgotten on earth, but we'll be remembered in heaven.

CLOSING

Take time as a group (or as couples) to pray in some of the following directions:

- "Father, we thank you for our ancestors, those who have gone before us, especially _____, _____, and _____. Whether they left a legacy of faith, or whether they simply lived and had offspring, we honor their role in your providential creation of our own family."
- "Lord, forgive us for the energy we have wasted and the hours we have let slip past by focusing on our own significance rather than living to serve you and draw others to you. Please renew our vision and commitment to seek first the kingdom of God rather than live for earthly acclaim."
- "Our Father, let us now spend some time in silence so that you can point out, by your Holy Spirit, faulty attitudes, pursuits, actions, expenditures, habits, activities, or anything else that is taking us away from your eternal priorities. Please reveal these to us and grant us hearts that are willing to change."
- "Jesus, we pray that you will be with our family several generations hence. We ask that the legacy of our family be _____, _____, and _____. Help us to raise our kids now in such a way as to pass on and preserve that legacy."

BETWEEN SESSIONS

On your own, or as a couple, read the following devotion in the next couple of days to further reflect on the lessons you have learned in this session.

DEVOTION: CREATING TIME

"For I have chosen him, so that he will direct his children and his household after him to keep the way of the LORD." (Genesis 18:19)

As part of my morning devotions, I pulled down a commentary on 2 Corinthians. A receipt for the book fell out, and I discovered that I had purchased this commentary two decades prior, in December of 1984, at the Regent College Bookstore.

In December of 1984, I had been married for just six months. Lisa and I didn't have any children — and frankly, I'm surprised I had enough money to actually buy a commentary. But there it was — incontrovertible proof.

My mind wandered to how the next two and a half decades passed. Over 9,000 days had slipped by. Some were put to good use; some, I'm sure, were wasted.

But they had all passed. They were gone. They would never come back.

Kelsey, my youngest daughter, has just graduated from high school. She served as a "mother hen" of her cross country team, showing great leadership. Her school principal told me how respected she was by the staff. In mere weeks, she'll move to Texas to go to college.

My son is finishing up an internship in New York City, will return this fall to school in Indiana, and will then spend a semester studying abroad in London.

My oldest daughter should finish her studies at a Christian college in Canada next spring. She aspires to serve with a Christian ministry that works in developing countries.

Three children.

Three different schools.

Three different countries.

When people say they don't have "time" for more children, they completely misunderstand God's creation. In one sense, children create more time by expanding our impact beyond our own direct efforts. Twenty years ago, there was just my wife and me, but now, through God's plan of procreation, a part of us will be walking, simultaneously, through three different educational institutions and living in three different countries.

Having children is a humble acceptance of our own limitations. We can only be in one place at one time. We only have so many days to live on this earth, and then we die. But when we give up some of our time, we create decades for others to live their lives and use their time for the glory of God. Raising three children to serve God for (under his providence) seven to eight decades is the most productive work we can do, the most efficient use of our time.

As you take time out of your busy life to invest in conceiving a child, feeding a child, cleaning a child, raising a child, and then training that child, you're creating something that no scientist could ever hope to engineer: you're setting into motion seven or eight decades of a human life.

But when we are so filled with our own importance that we refuse to have children for selfish reaons, or to raise the children we already have, we are shrinking our lives and actually limiting our own influence.

For today, may the mundane tasks of parenting take on a new wonder as you realize that God has chosen you to direct your children and your household after you to keep the way of the Lord.

RECOMMENDED READING

In preparation for session 5, please read chapter 3 of Sacred Parenting, *"The Gold behind the Guilt."*

Notes

SESSION 5

THE GOLD BEHIND THE GUILT

God uses even our inadequacies for his glory and purpose.

INTRODUCTION

Roger Bannister was the first runner to break the four-minute mile. Years before, many thought such a time was humanly impossible, but now even high school students occasionally dip below this mark.

Fifty years after he achieved his historic feat, Roger reflected on what motivated him — and what motivates many people today. He says it is a "universal truth" that "most of us find effort and struggle deeply satisfying, harnessing almost primeval instincts to fight, to survive. It gives us all a challenge, a sense of purpose." He goes on to describe the "profoundly satisfying effort in thought, feeling and hard work necessary to achieve this success."[1]

I was particularly struck when Roger said that such a struggle, though noble, "is increasingly difficult to find ... in our restricted twenty-first century lives."

It's true — there are very few places on this globe left to explore. Women and men by the scores have plunged to the depths of the oceans, and hundreds have now scaled Everest's heights. Few of us could ever imagine setting a new world record in the mile or marathon, and there are very few things we can do that haven't been done dozens if not hundreds of times already.

But what takes more effort, what demands more internal courage, fortitude, perseverance, and all the intellectual skill we can muster, than marriage and parenting? The work necessary to achieve success as a spouse and parent isn't just difficult — sometimes it seems downright impossible. Bannister ran twenty-five miles a week for ten years to achieve his goal, but a single decade doesn't even get a child into her teens, while a mere decade for marriage is normally no more than 20 percent of its whole if divorce doesn't bring it to an artificial end.

Certainly, we can agree with Roger that such a struggle harnesses "almost primeval instincts to fight, to survive." In even the most difficult of relationships, there is something within us that wants to make this marriage work, that keeps us from giving up on our children, that motivates us to push past the pain and find a way to keep loving.

Because parenting is so difficult, we are going to fail in certain aspects. For every Roger Bannister who breaks a milestone world record, there are thousands who fall short, people we never read about, but many of them tried just as hard as, perhaps even harder than, Roger himself. And still they failed.

It takes tremendous courage to undergo a task that you know will reveal your limitations, weak spots in your character, and occasional lapses of wisdom. That's why many people have run from the difficulty of family life and sought other, easier accomplishments — like becoming a scratch golfer, climbing Mount Everest, or running for the presidency of the United States. But let us overcome our personal fears as a climber overcomes his terror of heights on Mount Everest; let us push past our weariness as a cyclist keeps pedaling up the Alps during the Tour de France. Let us do what others refuse to do, what others fail to do: let us be fully married; let us stay involved in our kids' lives; let us, in spite of our sin, our lack of experience, our weaknesses, and our pain, build a family that honors God.

Our efforts will not be exalted on the sports pages or even mentioned in the gossip columns. We won't be interviewed on television or celebrated on the covers of magazines, and our own children will likely recount our failures.

But here's the thing: God has made us in such a way that difficulty is the doorway to satisfaction. If something is easily done, it may bring some little degree of pleasure, but it will not produce much sense of reward. Our family represents the greatest challenge we will ever face, but at the end, if we don't give up, if we face our sin, failures, and limitations, we will find that our imperfect families represent our most enduring pleasure, a supreme satisfaction and joy.

Before You Watch the Video

Share one or two parental failures that are legendary in your family. Next, share one or two things you wish you were better at as a parent.

DVD Teaching Notes

Guilt as a universal experience of parenting

How parenting reveals our inadequacies and limitations

We are not called to be _____; we are called to be
_____.

John the Baptist

Scriptural "heroes"

The "positive" side of our limitations
Weakness on our part can actually become _____
when we use it to transfer _____
to _____.

Training future servants in God's kingdom

Training our children to deal with their disappointment in us

The Samuel Syndrome

God's great risk

DVD DISCUSSION

1. Recount the parental failures you shared at the beginning of the group time, before you watched the video. Having heard what you just heard, how do you think God might be able to use those failures to build you up as a parent and to bring glory to himself?

2. Gary mentions in the video how there is always something we can do better, or more of, as a parent — read more, pray more, talk more, prepare our kids better financially, educationally, spiritually, etc. Talk about how unfair it is to compare another parent's strength with your weakness. Next, talk about how you can be *encouraged* by the positive (often convicting) examples of other parents rather than *discouraged*.

3. Have you ever aspired to be the "best parent in the world"? What are the dangers of such a goal?

We are not raising robots; we are shepherding image bearers of the Creator God who live with the freedom of choice, their own wills, and a personal responsibility of their own. It seems to me that we tend to take too much credit for kids who turn out good, and too much blame for kids who turn out bad.

4. Discuss practical ways in which remembering that we are called to be "messengers," and not "Messiahs," can transform the way we look at our failures, limitations, and struggles.

5. Does it surprise you how deeply flawed so many biblical heroes were? What does this tell us about the kind of people God chooses to use?

6. Discuss some ways we can train our kids to handle their eventual disappointment in our particular parental weaknesses. How can we use these limitations to point our children to God and to transfer their allegiance from us to him?

7. When is it unwise to share past failures with our children? What are the guiding principles behind what we share, and when, keeping in mind that we are called to always do what serves them and their love for God?

8. How does it make you feel that God, knowing full well your weaknesses and limitations, nevertheless took the great risk of letting you raise one (or several) of his children? How might this affect the way you relate to God, worship God, and serve God?

Acknowledge your guilt, and then thank God that he has made provision for your guilt. Confess that you have fallen short as a parent, but then expend just as much energy worshiping the God who forgives and who will show mercy to you in your failings. And then apply that same mercy to your children and your own parents.

9. Throughout this series we have stressed raising children "out of reverence for God." How does this rubric affect the way we should look at parental guilt, limitations, and failures?

CLOSING

Take time as a group (or as couples) to pray in some of the following directions:

- "Father, thank you for showing your great love for us, that though you know we have weaknesses and failures and many limitations, you still entrust your children to us to love, to raise, and to teach about you. Help us remember that you do love us, in spite of our sin, and help us live in a spirit of grace, forgiveness, acceptance, and affirmation. Please use our role as parents to regularly remind us of this deep truth."

- "Lord, forgive us for the energy we have wasted trying to impress our children with our own strength, instead of focusing on how we can train our children to be impressed by *you*. We pray that our focus, every day, would be to live, speak, and act in such a way that our children grow to love you more and more, even if that means being more vulnerable about our own sin and past."

- "Dear God, forgive us for taking credit when our kids do well, and forgive us for assuming undue responsibility when our kids fail. Help us to remember that faithful parents may raise unfaithful children, and parents who make many mistakes sometimes have children who become champions of the faith. We don't understand why or how this works, but we humbly recognize your providence and call, and we pray that you will lead our children to serve and worship you."

- "Jesus, we want to lift up the following parents who are racked with guilt: _____. May the truth of this lesson be a healing balm to their souls and an encouragement to keep moving forward."

BETWEEN SESSIONS

On your own, or as a couple, read the following devotion in the next couple of days to further reflect on the lessons you have learned in this session.

DEVOTION: A PARENT'S AGONY

"A sword will pierce your own soul too." (Luke 2:35)

The coming of Jesus carried both glorious and frightening news. Though this wasn't known to the world at large, on a cosmic level Jesus' entrance was neither an anonymous nor a safe birth. It was a direct challenge to the god of this world; of course Satan would rise up and oppose him with all his terrible might.

Make no mistake: that quiet birth in Bethlehem was the first shot fired in a celestial war. Jesus was born to die. He came to win a majestic but costly victory.

These twin realities — certain hope, fierce opposition — are no less present in our families, churches, and communities today. And parents are often caught in the middle of this celestial battle. Because we care so much about our children's welfare — including their eternal welfare — our own souls will feel pierced. Raising children is not a "safe" occupation.

Looking on the baby Jesus, Simeon marveled at what the child would be, but then changed his tone completely by warning Mary, "A sword will pierce your own soul too" (Luke 2:35). John Calvin sees this as a gracious act of mercy: "This warning must have contributed greatly to fortify the mind of the holy virgin, and to prevent her from being overwhelmed with grief, when she came to those distressing struggles, which she had to undergo. Though her faith was agitated and tormented by various temptations, yet her sorest battle was with the cross: for Christ might appear to be utterly destroyed. She was not overwhelmed with grief; but it would have required a heart of stone not to be deeply wounded: for the patience of the saints differs widely from stupidity."[1]

Of course, Mary's pain was unique, just as she raised a uniquely perfect child. But the notion that there will be great pride watching our children grow up, and times of great grief, is universal for all parents. We need to be reminded of this, indeed, to even expect it, lest we be caught off guard. As Calvin puts it, "The patience of the saints differs widely from stupidity." It is "stupid" to assume we can be parents without great pains.

Unlike for Mary, sometimes our grief will arise through our children's floundering. They may question their faith; if so, we will likely blame ourselves for it. Our children may go through a time of rebellion—and we'll bear the guilt, however justly or unjustly that guilt is deserved ("If only we had prayed more, taught more, been a better example").

It is a lie to assume that even if you did everything right, you could have avoided this pain. Mary raised a perfect son but still had to watch that perfect son be torn apart in front of her own eyes. At his birth she was given great news: "Your son is the Messiah!" And then she was delivered frightening news: "A sword will pierce your soul too."

Like Mary, we need to be warned, so here it is: parents, prepare to be pierced.

Parenting isn't about us; it's about him—and he is being attacked. Our children and families are one of the battlegrounds on which this ancient war will be waged. We are forewarned, and—according to Calvin—being forewarned, we are forearmed.

RECOMMENDED READING

In preparation for session 6, please read chapter 12 of Sacred Parenting, *"Sacrifice."*

Notes

SESSION 6

THE SWEET SIDE OF SACRIFICE

Raising children trains us for a fundamental Christian attitude: living in the spirit of sacrifice.

INTRODUCTION

Last April, I got to meet Dick Hoyt, a man famous to many runners. Dick's son Rick was born with cerebral palsy, the result of an umbilical cord wrapped around his neck at birth. Rick was severely disabled, unable to communicate at all, until Dick finally convinced a doctor to rig up a system whereby Rick could communicate through "typing" messages by moving his eyes and head.

Dick was excited to finally be able to "talk" with his son, but was somewhat taken aback when his son soon asked Dick to "run" a five-mile race. Dick was a self-described "couch potato." He couldn't remember running five blocks, much less five miles, but he wanted to serve his son, so he did it — and nearly collapsed at the end. This was in the days long before there were specialized running strollers. Dick was pushing an actual wheelchair.

As he stumbled to the finish, Dick thought to himself, "Finally, it's over," but one of the first messages Rick typed out after that experience was, "This was the only time I didn't feel disabled."

Dick was moved, as any father would be, and wanted to re-create that experience for his boy, so they began doing 5ks together, then 10ks, and then began an incredible run of more than 25 consecutive Boston marathons. One year Dick got really crazy and did an Ironman triathlon — a 2.4-mile swim, a 112-mile bike ride, and a 26.2-mile run, all the while either pulling, carrying, or pushing Rick.

Many have seen the movie of Dick's heroics, but fewer know that, several years ago, Dick visited the doctor because he wasn't feeling well. The medical personnel ran some tests and called him on the phone as he was driving away.

"Where are you headed?" the nurse asked.

"The gym," Dick said.

"No, you're not," the nurse responded. "You've had a heart attack."

Later, the doctor explained that, given his genetic makeup and history, Dick probably would have been dead a decade or so sooner if he hadn't been in such good shape. That's when Dick realized something profound: all those years of getting in shape so that he could push his son through races ended up doing more for him than it did for his son. His sacrifice for his son literally saved his own life.

Spiritually speaking, the same can be true for us: learning to make sacrifices for our children can build in us the absolutely necessary attitude of a believer. It can "save" us from our selfishness and self-absorption. Jesus calls his disciples to "take up their cross" daily, and Paul describes the Christian life in Romans 12:1 as becoming "living sacrifices." Ill-informed or spiritually immature people resent sacrifice of any kind, and often become hardened when forced to face it. Christian parents — if they surrender their hearts to God — can ride every act of sacrifice to new depths of Christian maturity. We were given spiritual birth through Christ's great act of sacrifice, and we can continue to grow by accepting the call to sacrifice in return.

It's particularly brilliant on God's part to school us in the art of sacrifice by giving us children whom we love so much — and who require so much sacrifice to raise.

BEFORE YOU WATCH THE VIDEO

If you were talking to a young, childless couple and they asked you, "What are the sacrifices involved in parenting that we should be prepared to make?" what would you say to them?

DVD TEACHING NOTES

A faithful heart of sacrifice

Gary's attitude — "I'm willing to act like a Christian as long as it doesn't cost me anything" — versus King David's attitude — "I will not sacrifice to the LORD my God burnt offerings that cost me nothing" (2 Samuel 24:24)

Christianity was birthed in sacrifice.

We are called to be "living sacrifices" (Romans 12:1).

SACRED PARENTING PARTICIPANT'S GUIDE

Parental sacrifice

2 Corinthians 12:14 – 15 — "Children should not have to save up for their parents, but parents for their children. So I will very gladly spend for you everything I have and expend myself as well."

The great transformation

Paul makes himself a slave (1 Corinthians 9:19).

Paul is awed by Christ's sacrifice.

- "I have been crucified with Christ and I no longer live, but Christ lives in me. The life I live in the body, I live by faith in the Son of God, who loved me and gave himself for me." (Galatians 2:20)
- "[God] did not spare his own Son, but gave him up for us all." (Romans 8:32)
- "The Lord Jesus Christ ... gave himself for our sins." (Galatians 1:3 – 4)
- "Christ loved us and gave himself up for us." (Ephesians 5:2)
- "Christ Jesus ... gave himself as a ransom for all." (1 Timothy 2:5 – 6)
- "Our great God and Savior, Jesus Christ ... gave himself for us to redeem us." (Titus 2:13 – 14)
- "Husbands, love your wives, just as Christ loved the church *and gave himself up for her.*" (Ephesians 5:25, emphasis added)

Our small acts of parental sacrifice can tune us in to God's amazing sacrifice.

Parenting as a season

DVD DISCUSSION

1. If you were to put your current attitude on a spectrum between David's and Gary's, where would you place yourself?

Gary	David
I'm willing	I will not
to act like	sacrifice to the
a Christian	Lord my God
as long as it	something
doesn't cost	that costs me
me anything.	nothing.

2. If you were to plot the typical life journey from selfishness to self-less service and then to sacrifice, what would you expect to see along the way? That is, describe the kinds of experiences God might lead us through to shape our hearts, change our attitudes, and transform our thinking so that we might truly become "living sacrifices." How might God specifically use parenting to shape us in this direction?

Kids' needs are rarely "convenient." ... To raise them well will require daily sacrifices of many kinds.... Once we have children, we cannot act and dream as though we had remained childless.

3. Describe the difference between someone who focuses on holiness as a list of things they avoid doing and someone who views holiness as a life of service to God through serving others (i.e., sacrifice). How do we recapture the spirit of holiness expressed by Paul in 1 Corinthians 9:19?

4. Have you ever had to clearly sacrifice something to live out your faith? What did it feel like? Looking back on that event, how do you believe that act helped you to grow?

5. Is there anything now that you believe you need to let go of in order to be a more involved parent, but you're having a difficult time accepting the sacrifice? Is it financial? Time related? Work related? A hobby? What can we do to embrace obedience when such sacrifices present themselves?

Sacrifice and the corresponding virtue of humility aren't built on giant gestures as much as they are forged with consistent, thoughtful actions of an everyday nature: a dad choosing to play a board game with his little girl instead of turning on the television; a woman making sure she's home for dinner instead of staying late at the office; parents who enjoy a hobby far less frequently than they'd like for the sake of spending more time with their children.

CLOSING

Take time as a group (or as couples) to pray in some of the following directions:

- "Lord Jesus, thank you for offering yourself as the perfect sacrifice on our behalf. We pray we would be like Paul, in constant awe that you would give yourself up for us. Let us never grow callous to the extreme price you paid to reconcile us to yourself."
- "Father, forgive us for selfishly receiving your blessings and then resenting it when you ask us to sacrifice some of those blessings on behalf of others. We pray that we would be 'living sacrifices' in the future, gratefully receiving whatever you give, but just as eagerly letting go of everything you ask us to."
- "Dear God, we sit before you in silence, giving you an opportunity to speak to us about something you might be asking us to sacrifice even today, on behalf of our families or the kingdom work you are calling us to."

IN THE COMING DAYS

On your own, or as a couple, read the following devotion in the next couple of days to further reflect on the lessons you have learned in this session.

DEVOTION: THE WORTH BEHIND THE WORK

"Sow your seed in the morning, and at evening let not your hands be idle, for you do not know which will succeed, whether this or that." (Ecclesiastes 11:6)

One summer, because of two book deadlines and an international speaking trip, I inadvertently scheduled myself out of any summer vacation. I was already exhausted before I left for the African continent, and the brutal thirty-three hours (one way) of travel time — including twenty-one hours of being in the air — took a good week to recover from when I finally returned home, except that I had agreed to speak at another conference just two days after I got back.

When I finally carved out a week in the early fall and was able to pray through my year, my frustrations, my tiredness, all of it, I was shocked when I believe God began to give me some of his perspective. I'm at a point in my career where, if I were single and childless, I could support myself on about four hours of work a day — while taking the summers off. That might sound shocking initially, but I believe it's true for many men, if not the majority. If we didn't have families to support, most of us could make do in an apartment with rather low overhead and work much less than we do.

This realization put a face on the long days, the no-vacation summers, the travel, and the tiredness; that "face" is my wife's, my two daughters', and my son's. And in an unmistakable way, I believed God gave me a glimpse of his pleasure that I was willing to work so hard to take care of four other people who are very precious to him.

My work is minuscule compared to that of the single moms or even married working moms who not only put in long hours at their job, but then sacrifice almost all their leisure time to stay connected with their children when they get home. They have to listen to work-related problems all day long and then come home and listen to their kids' problems in the evening. They often stay up late to spend time with their kids, but have to rise early to earn money for their kids.

This is a tremendous sacrifice, but when we support our families, we give God great pleasure. He is passionate about the welfare of those we love. He delights when a wife is blessed with tokens of affection, when children are well fed and clothed, when a husband is encouraged and supported, because each wife, each husband, each son or daughter is one of his dearly loved children.

Have you ever thought about how much pleasure you give to God by sacrificing on behalf of your family? Our individual sacrifices will necessarily be different, but I'm coming to believe that loving my family well gives God more pleasure than perhaps anything else that I do.

What I'm saying is that when you cut down your hours or even quit your job to spend time with your kids (or conversely, take on a second job to provide for your kids); when you choose to care for a disabled child or elderly parent at home; when you give up the shopping trip to pay for a child's visit to the dentist, these sacrifices aren't made in a vacuum. They are offerings to God, every bit as sweet and pleasing to the Lord as the check we place in the basket on Sunday morning.

The pleasure we can give God in this way is tremendous. My kids are getting old enough now that I'm thinking about their future marriage partners. I really don't care if Graham marries a blonde or a brunette. I won't care if she's an extrovert or an introvert. It won't matter to me if she majored in English literature or accounting or even if she chose not to get a college degree. What will give me the most pleasure about her is seeing her love Graham well. She can't do anything else that would make me happier than being a loving wife to my son.

In the same way, whether my future sons-in-law are bankers, postal workers, teachers, CEOs, or professional athletes won't matter half as much to me, not even a tenth as much, as how well they love my daughters, Allison and Kelsey. If they treat my girls well and affectionately, if they honor and respect them, adore them, and cherish them, those two boys will make me the happiest father-in-law on earth.

Today, we can give God the same pleasure that these future sons-in-law and daughter-in-law may one day give me: we can love his children well.

Give God pleasure today. Make those sacrifices. Love his children. And every now and then, pause for a moment to bask in God's great affirmation. Revel in the pleasure he feels when one of his children becomes an avenue through which he can love an entire family.

Notes

Endnotes

Session 1

1. Dr. James Dobson, "Solid Answers," *Focus on the Family* magazine, July 2002, 5.
2. Iris Krasnow, *Surrendering to Motherhood: Losing Your Mind, Finding Your Soul* (New York: Hyperion, 1997), 1–2.

Session 2

1. Martin Luther, "The Estate of Marriage," in *The Book of Marriage*, ed. Dana Mack and David Blankenhorn (Grand Rapids: Eerdmans, 2001), 373.

Session 3

1. Cited in H. W. Brands, *The First American: The Life and Times of Benjamin Franklin* (New York: Random House, 2000), 309.
2. Ibid., 309.

Session 5

1. Roger Bannister, *The Four-Minute Mile: 50th Anniversary Edition* (Guilford, Conn.: Lyons Press, 2004), viii.
2. John Calvin, *Calvin's Commentaries, vol. 7, The Gospels* (Grand Rapids: Associated Publishers and Authors, Inc., n.d.), 66.

Sacred Parenting

How Raising Children Shapes Our Souls

Gary Thomas, Bestselling Author of Sacred Marriage

Parenting is a school for spiritual formation—and our children are our teachers. The journey of caring for, rearing, training, and loving our children will profoundly alter us forever.

Sacred Parenting is unlike any other parenting book you have ever read. This is not a "how-to" book that teaches you ways to discipline your kids or help them achieve their full potential. Instead of discussing how parents can change their kids, Sacred Parenting turns the tables and demonstrates how God uses our kids to change us.

You've read all the method books. Now take a step back and receive some much-needed inspiration. You'll be encouraged by stories that tell how other parents handled the challenges and difficulties of being a parent—and how their children transformed their relationship with God. Sacred Parenting affirms the spiritual value of being a parent, showing you the holy potential of the parent-child relationship.

Available in stores and online!

ZONDERVAN®
.com

Sacred Marriage

DVD Curriculum

What If God Designed Marriage To Make Us Holy More Than To Make Us Happy?

Gary Thomas

Your marriage is much more than a union between you and your spouse. It is a spiritual discipline ideally suited to help you know God more fully and intimately. *Sacred Marriage* shifts the focus from marital enrichment to spiritual enrichment in ways that can help you love your mate more. Whether it is delightful or difficult, your marriage can become a doorway to a closer walk with God.

Everything about your marriage—everything from the history you and your spouse create, to the love you share, to the forgiveness you both offer and seek by turn—is filled with the capacity to help you grow in Christ's character. This six-session, small group DVD curriculum and separate participant's guide will equip you to love God more passionately, reflect the nature of his Son more precisely, and fulfill God's overarching purpose for your marriage.

Available in stores and online!

Devotions for Sacred Parenting

A Year of Weekly Devotions for Parents

Gary Thomas, Bestselling Author of Sacred Marriage

Raising children shapes the parent every bit as much as parents shape their children.

Raising children is a sacred calling—and not for the faint of heart. In *Devotions for Sacred Parenting*, the author of *Sacred Parenting* continues the conversation and contemplates the soul-transforming journey of being a parent.

With all new material, fifty-two devotions explore the spiritual dynamics of parenting. These life-related devotions are creative, fresh, and encouraging, inspiring mothers and fathers to look at parenting from a different perspective—as a holy and high calling from God, and as an opportunity to grow spiritually as you strive to raise godly children. *Devotions for Sacred Parenting* helps you understand how God is parenting you as you parent your children.

Available in stores and online!

Share Your Thoughts

With the Author: Your comments will be forwarded to the author when you send them to *zauthor@zondervan.com*.

With Zondervan: Submit your review of this book by writing to *zreview@zondervan.com*.

Free Online Resources at
www.zondervan.com

Zondervan AuthorTracker: Be notified whenever your favorite authors publish new books, go on tour, or post an update about what's happening in their lives at www.zondervan.com/authortracker.

Daily Bible Verses and Devotions: Enrich your life with daily Bible verses or devotions that help you start every morning focused on God. Visit www.zondervan.com/newsletters.

Free Email Publications: Sign up for newsletters on Christian living, academic resources, church ministry, fiction, children's resources, and more. Visit www.zondervan.com/newsletters.

Zondervan Bible Search: Find and compare Bible passages in a variety of translations at www.zondervanbiblesearch.com.

Other Benefits: Register yourself to receive online benefits like coupons and special offers, or to participate in research.

ZONDERVAN®

ZONDERVAN.com/
AUTHORTRACKER
follow your favorite authors